This Sketchbook Belongs to

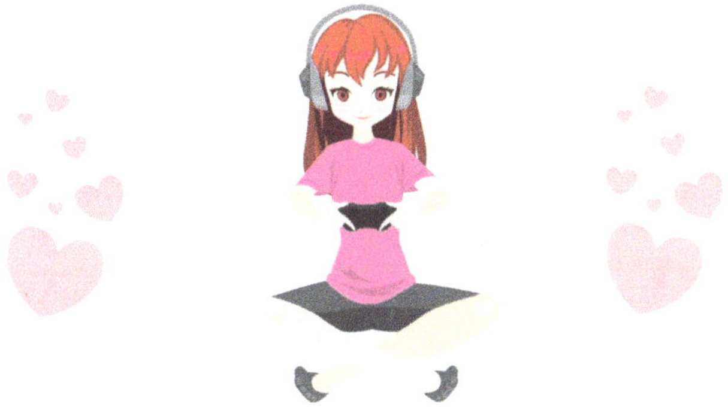

www.ingramcontent.com/pod-product-compliance
Lightning Source LLC
Chambersburg PA
CBHW070602220526
45467CB00003B/1270
9781716130823